THE CASE of the WATER CRISIS

You will know the truth and the truth will set you free.

Art: Mychailo Kazybrid

Script: Ed Chatelier

Lettering and Color and Cover Design: Richard Thomas

Creative Concept: EDGE GROUP Creative Media Agency

contact: edgesword@yahoo.com

+447905960775

THANKS TO:

Alexander Otte UNESCO

Michiko Tanaka UNESCO, Ian Denison UNESCO

Thanks to UNESCO.

First published in Great Britain in 2016

by Edge Group,
138 Grove Hall Court
London, NW8, UK

Copyright © UNESCO and Edge G3 Limited, 2016

DISCLAIMER

The designations employed and the presentations of material throughout this publication do not imply the expression of any opinion whatsoever on the part of UNESCO concerning the legal status of any country, territory, city or area or of its authorities, or concerning the delimitation of it's frontiers or boundaries.

The ideas and opinions expressed in this publication are those of the authors; they are not necessarily of UNESCO and do not commit the Organisation.

ISBN:

978-0-9569731-8-4

FACT: TODAY, AN ESTIMATED 884 MILLION PEOPLE CAN'T GET SAFE DRINKING WATER.

FACT: IT IS ESTIMATED THAT AT LEAST 4000 CHILDREN DIE EACH DAY BECAUSE THEY CAN'T EASILY GET CLEAN WATER.

FACT: 70% OF OUR PLANET'S SURFACE IS COVERED BY WATER. BUT 97.5% OF THIS IS SALT WATER THAT WE CAN'T DRINK.

FACT: ALTHOUGH 2.5% IS FRESH WATER MOST OF THIS IS TRAPPED IN ICE CAPS AND IN THE GROUND.

FACT: THE 1% OF DIRECTLY ACCESSIBLE FRESH WATER IS IN RIVERS, RESERVOIRS AND UNDERGROUND, AND SO IS NOT FOUND EVERYWHERE AROUND THE WORLD.

FACT: INTERESTINGLY HUMAN BEINGS CONSIST OF 60-70% WATER. MOST OF THE REST IS PROTEIN (20%) AND MINERALS.

FACT: THE HUMAN BRAIN IS MADE UP OF 75% WATER.

FACT: WHILE IN URBAN SOCIETY USE 140 LITRES PER DAY. THEY ONLY NEED 20 LITRES.

FACT: UNWASHED HANDS CAN CARRY BACTERIA, WHICH CAN CAUSE SICKNESS.

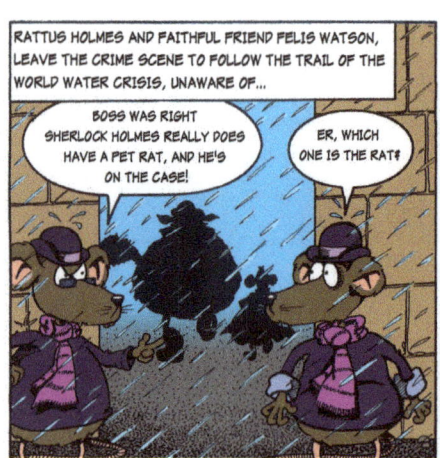

FACT: TOXIC WASTE DUMPED IN RIVERS AND SEAS POISONS PRECIOUS WATER SUPPLIES.

FACT: GLOBAL WARMING IS CAUSING POLAR ICE CAPS, SHELVES AND GLACIERS TO MELT PRECIPITATING REGIONAL CRISES.

FACT: HALF OF THE WATER IN MANY TOWNS IS LOST THROUGH LEAKING PIPES.

FACT: MANY CITIES WATER SUPPLIES DEPEND ON RESERVOIR LEVELS. OVERUSE AND LACK OF RAIN CAN PUT WHOLE CITIES UNDER STRESS.

FACT: INDUSTRIES NEED TO HAVE RESPONSIBLE POLICIES THAT SAFEGUARD THE ECOSYSTEMS THEY OPERATE IN – AND OFTEN DEPEND ON.

FACT: RIVERS CAN TRANSFER UPSTREAM POLLUTION TO COMMUNITIES DOWNSTREAM.

FACT: THE WATER CRISIS IS INTIMATELY TIED TO WATER MISMANAGEMENT, CLIMATE CHANGE, POLLUTION, DEFORESTATION ETC...

FACT: WHILE A HUMAN BEING CAN LIVE A MONTH WITHOUT FOOD, HE OR SHE CAN ONLY SURVIVE A FEW DAYS WITHOUT WATER.

www.ingramcontent.com/pod-product-compliance
Lightning Source LLC
Chambersburg PA
CBHW040733020526
44112CB00059B/2956